Broken Reed
The Lords of Gower and King John

Behold, you are trusting in Egypt, that broken reed of a staff,
which will pierce the hand of any man who leans on it.
(Isaiah 36:6)

Ann Marie Thomas

Alina Publishing
Swansea

Contents

About the author

Writing poetry and making up stories since she was a child, she only started to write seriously when her children were grown. Her main ambition was to write science fiction, but along the way she got fascinated by local history and distracted by a major stroke. However, she wrote poetry about her stroke and spent her recovery writing a local history book. Taking early retirement gave her more time to concentrate on her writing.

Connect with her online:
Blog: https://annmariethomas.me.uk/
Twitter: @AnnMThomas80
Facebook: http://on.fb.me/1MUd6Kb
Email: amt.tetelestai@gmail.com
LinkedIn: http://linkd.in/1MUdsAv
GoodReads: http://bit.ly/21nG4Jv
Also available on Amazon for Kindle and in multiple ebook formats on Smashwords.com

Introduction

Map of the Angevin Empire

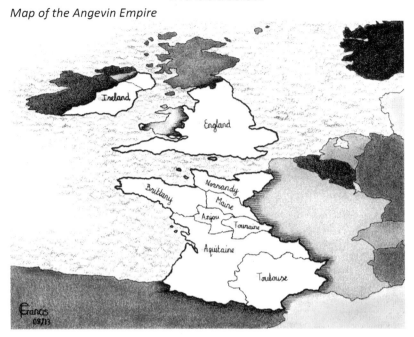

Most people's knowledge of history is pretty patchy, and often influenced by the odd television documentary they might have seen and some frequently inaccurate films. Many of us didn't enjoy history lessons in school, especially the ones involving boring lists of kings and laws and wars. But history is about people – their lives, their loves, their decisions – and not always the kings and famous names.

Swansea and the Gower peninsular is a tiny area on the South Wales coast, currently an Area of Outstanding Natural Beauty. In the 18th and 19th centuries it was a major world centre for coal mining and metal smelting. But the area is full of Norman castles – Swansea Castle ruins are right in the city centre. Researching what life was like when these castles were in use led me to the story of the heir to the Lordship of Gower whose little rebellion ended up toppling Edward II from the English throne. That story, about Alina de Breos, was told in my book *Alina, The White Lady of Oystermouth*. Now here's another astounding story about another de Breos and the fallout from his life a century earlier. Since so many of the de Breoses were called William, I have numbered them to distinguish between them.

The de Breos Lords of Gower were involved in virtually every major event in English history for three hundred years after the Norman conquest, yet their name very rarely appears in historical accounts. When Richard the Lionheart was fatally wounded in 1199 while besieging a castle in France, William III de Breos, 4th Lord of Bramber, one of the foremost Norman warriors, was there among his fighting barons. At Richard's death William immediately switched his allegiance to support the claim of Richard's brother John to the throne. In fact, John's return to England was via William's port of Shoreham in Sussex.[i] He was richly rewarded for his support. John's gifts made William one of the richest barons in England — yet history hardly mentions him.

In medieval times power came through land, and a system of fealty where a vassal would pledge faithfulness to his lord in return for protection. The more powerful barons would often rule many estates, with the individual estates ruled by lesser lords. Some lords ruled more than one estate as a vassal of different barons. If those barons fought, their vassals found themselves in a difficult position. Which baron should they support? If the wrong baron won, they would be counted a traitor.

The Angevin kings ruled England and territories in France and were historically vassals of the king of France, though they claimed to rule in their own right. The King of France was continually trying to bring them to heel, either by direct conquest or by subverting their vassals. So there was a constant battle to keep power. Lands were given to people as rewards, for favour, or in an attempt to balance power so no one vassal held too much land.

King John gave William lands for all these reasons, and favoured him in land disputes with other barons, trusting him as one of his inner circle. He was the only one of the de Breos line to unify their lands and to hold such a vast number of estates. He profited under Henry II and Richard, but it was under John he rose to greatest prominence. Yet it was under John he fell, suddenly out of favour and hounded to death. One writer called him 'a broken reed'[ii].

History depicts Richard the Lionheart as the handsome hero and his brother John as an ugly tyrant, but that's not the whole picture. Tall, handsome and heroic Richard may have been, but out of his whole ten-year reign he spent less than six months in England and never bothered to learn English[iii]. Yet he was charismatic enough to win the people's loyalty, such that they raised enormous sums of money for him to go on crusade, and to pay his ransom after he was captured on the way home. And he chose able men to look after his empire while he was away.

His brother John on the other hand was a stocky, red-haired man of medium height and no hero. He failed to win the trust and loyalty of the most powerful men in the land, which had disastrous results. His behaviour was unpredictable, and he could be childish and cruel. But he was highly intelligent and shrewd, and an able governor and administrator[iv]. One wonders how popular Richard would have been if he had had to stay and rule England in person, and how successful John would have been with the barons on his side and a more stable temperament.

And where might William III have been, and his descendants, if he had stayed in John's favour?

Chapter 1 – King John's Background
King John & coat of arms in the shadow of Richard I

Francis
08/13

John was to become both the patron of William III de Breos and his nemesis. To understand William's story it's important to know something about this king and the politics of the time. John was born on Christmas Eve 1166, the youngest child of Henry II and Eleanor of Aquitaine, a powerful woman in her own right. Henry II was the founder of the Plantagenet dynasty of English kings. The last of the line was Richard III whose body was dug up in a Leicester car park in 2012. Henry was also the overlord of the Angevin empire — he was lord of more land in France than the King of France himself, Louis VII. His territory stretched all the way from the Scottish border and Ireland to the Pyrenees mountains south of France[v].

The trouble was, he had so much land, he spent all his reign trying to hold it, waging war in places like Brittany, Normandy, Wales, Scotland and even Ireland[vi], as one magnate or another tried to gain more independence or more land. And he was always at odds with the King of France. John would become the last of the Angevin kings, as during his reign all the lands in France were lost.

In medieval times noble families were not like families today. Babies were handed over to wet-nurses, who usually became their nannies and looked after them for many years. The family structure was not about parents and children as a unit, but about heirs to carry on the line. As the youngest child, John would have expected nothing – no lands or inheritance, hopefully just enough revenue from the king to live on. Another option was to go into the church.

Eleanor of Aquitaine was more involved with her children than was usual at the time, but she took a dislike to John, perhaps because he was conceived on one of Henry's brief infrequent visits. John's three older brothers, Henry, Richard and Geoffrey, had spent much time in childhood with both their parents, but for some reason John was packed off to Fontevraud Abbey at the age of three for five years[vii], leading historians to suggest he was maladjusted. Today it's thought he had mental health problems or even suffered autistic spectrum disorder. One commentator said, 'When all allowances for the bias of hostile witnesses have been made, what remains is a clear indication of manic-depressive behaviour, bipolar affective disorder ... – a diagnosis that would account for the violent mood swings and tempestuous rages'[viii]. All of which goes a long way to explaining his unpredictability and bad behaviour.

In an attempt to spread the responsibility for control of his vast lands and to prevent war between his sons after his death, Henry divided the territory between them and had his eldest son crowned during his lifetime, on 24 May 1170[ix]. His son was referred to as the Young King and Henry as the Old King, since they both had the same name. Richard was given Gascony and Poitou and inherited his mother Eleanor's territory of Aquitaine. Geoffrey was given Brittany. Henry hoped they would rule the empire as a friendly coalition.

However, the move made his three older sons long for power sooner and, encouraged by their mother, they continuously rebelled and tried to seize territory by force. They were supported by several of the English barons and King Louis, Henry's old enemy. The Young King died suddenly of fever on 11 June 1183. Geoffrey was riding in a tournament in Paris when he fell and was badly cut up by the horses' hooves. He contracted a fever and died on 19 August 1186[x]. Henry had to rethink his plans for John & Richard.

Things were further complicated by the birth of Geoffrey's son Arthur of Brittany the following March, who was now second in line to the throne – after Richard and before John. Everybody wanted the right to take care of the baby and influence his education. Things were heading towards war between Henry and Philip, the new French king, until the Pope sent a message to say Christian troops should be fighting in the Holy Land, not fighting each other. They couldn't work out terms for peace so they called a two-year truce[xi].

The truce was extended a few months, but as it was coming to an end Henry fell ill. Richard and Philip refused to believe it and began new attacks as soon as the truce ended. As castle after castle fell, Henry was forced to flee and eventually had to submit, pay homage to Philip and give Richard the kiss of peace. In pain from his fever, and humiliation from his defeat, Henry heard on 5 July 1189 his beloved John had gone over to the enemy, and sworn fealty to Philip. At this betrayal he lost the will to live[xii], and died on 6 July.

Richard moved at once to secure his hold on the Angevin empire, and release his mother from her latest captivity, making her temporary regent of England until he came. The Archbishop of Canterbury crowned Richard in Westminster Abbey on 3 September 1189[xiii].

Immediately Richard began making plans to go on Crusade. He had to ensure the security of the kingdom in his absence and raise the vast amount of money he would need to finance the expedition. He named his nephew Arthur of Brittany as his heir, hoping to keep John quiet by showering him with lordships, titles and revenues.

Richard went on Crusade with a great company. He distinguished himself in fighting and strategy, but coming home it was a different matter. He dismissed most of his men and travelled incognito with a small party. He was captured by Duke Leopold of Austria in December 1192[xiv].

The ransom asked for was 100,000 marks[xv] and various undertakings about marriage and goods. It put an enormous burden on not only England's treasury, but the people, who gave all they could to raise this huge amount. Once Richard was released he returned to England only briefly and then went to France to secure the Angevin lands. He met with Philip of France, and John, and declared John his heir[xvi]. But the fighting continued.

In the spring of 1199 Richard moved against the Vicomte of Limoges and the Count of Angoulême At the siege of Chalus-Chabrol he went to inspect the siegeworks without wearing his armour, and was shot by a crossbow. The wound turned gangrenous, and he died on 6 April[xvii]. All Richard's contemporaries were shocked and uncertain what to do, where to pledge their loyalty, who would be the next king.

John had spent the previous five years serving Richard as a soldier. He had won many people to his cause by his apparent reform, including his brother. But he still had to fight for his claim to the throne against Arthur of Brittany and Philip, King of France. He made first for Rouen, where he was invested as Duke of Normandy on 25 April, and then raised an army and razed Le Mans for the treason of supporting Arthur[xviii]. His mother ensured Aquitaine supported him, so he went to England to secure the crown before turning to the other areas in France which were opposed to him.

He was crowned in Westminster Abbey on Ascension Day, 25 May 1199.

John went from being the youngest son, expecting nothing and nothing expected of him, to King of England and the Angevin empire. His older brothers, and to some extent his father, had set him a bad example of how to be a king. It needed firm control, shrewd distribution of power to the right men in the right places, and cunning to play the political games.

Chapter 2 – The Rise & Fall of William III de Breos
The approximate extent of William's lands in Wales

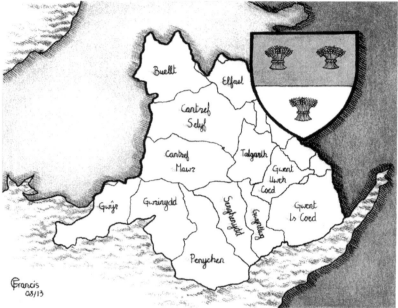

William III de Breos, 4th Lord of Bramber, came from a distinguished line of Norman barons, of which he was the pinnacle. No one before or after him had such a vast number of lands or wielded such influence. A favourite of King John, he consolidated the lands earned by his predecessors and gained many more. The greatest of his holdings were in Wales where he was lord over a vast swathe of land across mid and south Wales. Yet his very power and intimacy with the king proved to be his downfall, as John became suspicious of him and turned against him.

Gillaume de Briouze (d.c.1085) was a companion of William the Conqueror at the Battle of Hastings. The Briouze name comes from their estate in the village of Briouze-Saint-Gervais in southern Normandy[xix]. William awarded him estates in conquered England

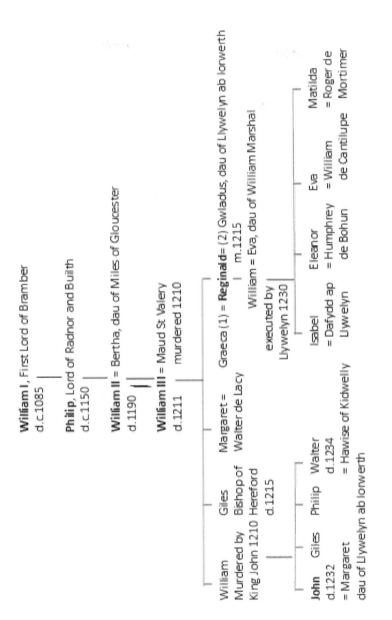

which made him one of the twenty wealthiest barons there. He had the whole of the Rape of Bramber (The word rape comes from the Old English word for rope, which was used to mark out territory). The Rape of Bramber was one of the six north-south sections into which West Sussex was divided[xx]. Gillaume's name was anglicised as William de Braose, which was later spelled Breuse or Breos. Locals in Gower today pronounce it 'Bruce'.

His son Philip (d.c.1150) became the first Lord of Builth and Radnor, the first de Breos holdings in Wales. There is evidence he went on the First Crusade[xxi], which was sent from Europe to try to regain the Holy Land lost to the Muslims. He became internationally recognised, referred to in a letter from the Archbishop of Canterbury to the Pope as an example of piety. After his death, his son William II inherited lands in Sussex, Devon and Wales.

William II, the 3rd Lord of Bramber, married Bertha, daughter of Miles of Gloucester, who had four brothers who were expected to inherit. But they all died childless and the inheritance was split between the daughters. William and Bertha got Brecon and Abergavenny, which gave them a vast block of territory in the Middle March of Wales. William was close to King Stephen and was in the escort for the defeated Empress Maud. He served King Henry II and was part of many of the king's expeditions in France. He was appointed sheriff of Hereford in 1173[xxii].

In 1175, however, William decided to avenge the death of his wife's brother, and caused quite a scandal. This was Henry Fitzmiles, third son of Miles of Gloucester, who was killed in battle by a Welsh leader, Seisyll ap Dyfnwal of Castle Arnallt, in 1165. William invited Seisyll and other Welsh leaders of Gwent to Abergavenny Castle. Some historians, including Gerald of Wales, say it was to hear the reading of a royal proclamation, some say it was to a Christmas Day feast of reconciliation. They all left their arms outside, as was the custom. William's men rose and murdered them all, including Seisyll's eldest son Gruffydd. Seisyll's wife attempted to escape with her seven-year-old son, Prince Cadwaladr, but William hunted them down and killed the son in his mother's armsxxiii.

This resulted in outrage and hostility from the Welsh, whom the kings were always trying to pacify. They named William 'The Ogre of Abergavenny'. William was forced to 'retire' from public life for this abuse. Gerald of Wales emphasised his subsequent great piety and generosity to the priories of Abergavenny and Brecon, presumably in an attempt to atone for his crime. Abergavenny was taken over by his son and heir, another William (III). Seven years later Seisyllt's surviving sons took their revenge by burning Abergavenny Castle down. The keep survived and William built a new castlexxiv.

William III, the 4th Lord of Bramber, inherited Bramber, Builth, Radnor, Brecknock and Abergavenny, and was already the strongest of the Marcher Barons. He fought beside King Richard many times, and held the office of Sheriff of Hereford for seven yearsxxv. He supported King John against Arthur of Brittany in his claim to the throne. As a reward for supporting John over Arthur, William III became very influential and part of John's intimate circle. He and his wife Maud de St Valery had at least sixteen childrenxxvi.

In 1202, he was fighting along with John to rescue the dowager Queen Eleanor, who was being besieged at Mirabeau by Arthur of Brittany and his supporters. John's forces were victorious, and during the battle William captured Arthur. John imprisoned Arthur's supporters in Corfe Castle and starved them to death. Arthur himself was imprisoned at Rouen, guarded by William.

For some time there were rumours about Arthur's fate, but the truth was kept hidden. Later it emerged that one night in 1203 John killed Arthur himself in a drunken rage and had his body tied to a stone and thrown in the River Seinexxvii. In February John gave William the Lordship of Gower (including the manors of Kilvey and Llan-dimore, which had been under disputexxviii). Some think this was to reward him for the capture of Arthur, some for the more sinister motive of buying his silence over Arthur's death.

In addition to Gower, John gave him Kington and the three castles of Skenfrith, Grosmont and Whitecastle in Gwent. He was also given custody of Glamorgan, Monmouth and Gwynllwg in return for large paymentsxxix. John even made him Lord of Limerick in Ireland. His honours reached their peak when he was made Sheriff of Hereford in 1206. The list of all his lands is enormous, listed in the endnotes[xxx].

In 1204 William III had fought for John when Philip of France attacked Normandy. England had been almost bankrupted by the cost of Richard's crusade and ransom, and as a result John didn't have the money to wage war as Philip did. Consequently, Normandy, homeland to many of the great barons in England, was lost to France. In the years that followed, many of the barons attempted to take lands in Wales and Ireland as compensation. John entrusted lands in Ireland to William in order to have support over there.

William's influence at court however, lasted only a few years. Having used his lands as a buffer against the Welsh, John became concerned he was becoming too powerful. He asked for money and William's sons as hostages to his loyalty. When William arrived home with the barons sent to collect, William's wife Maud refused. A strong-willed woman, she said she would not hand over her sons to a murderer, who had assassinated his own nephew, Arthur[xxxi]. The barons and their men were shocked and went back and told John. Maud speaking openly about John's secret sealed William's fate.

Later John would try to justify his actions. He wrote an open letter saying William had owed him a vast amount of money and had refused to hand over his lands as a forfeit for the debt. The kings raised money by taking payments for everything: inheritance rights, favourable judgements, marriage, even lands – John gave William many lands, but he was expected to pay for them all. As one of John's favourites, he probably didn't expect to pay all his debts[xxxii]. In fact John had already forgiven all the debts he owed to Henry II and Richard. It was a convenient way out for John, but it didn't explain the severity of his treatment of William.

One of William's sons was in trouble with John too. In 1207 the Pope selected Stephen Langton to be the new Archbishop of Canterbury, but John refused to accept him. In retaliation the Pope put England under an interdict, which meant no one in England could take part in any church rites, and excommunicated John. John promptly confiscated all church property. William's son Giles was bishop of Hereford, and was among the churchmen who fled to the safety of France with Stephen Langton.

John did call in a debt from William, and after a meeting, confiscated Brecon, Hay and Radnor and this time demanded William's grandsons as hostages. William agreed and then immediately launched a rebellion with his sons William IV and Reginald in an attempt to recapture the castles, which was unsuccessful. John dispossessed and outlawed William III in 1208. His wife Maud tried to placate John with a gift of Welsh white cattle, but to no avail[xxxiii].

The fall of William III left a vacuum in Wales, which was soon taken advantage of by the princes of Powys and Gwynedd, Gwenwynwyn and Llywelyn. William's sweep of land acted as a buffer between the Welsh and the Normans. Without William to keep the Welsh in check they quickly rebelled and John was forced to launch a campaign to crush them.

William fled with his family to his estate in Ireland. The Lacy brothers, Huw and Walter, were becoming powerful in Ireland, and when William Marshal, 1st Earl of Pembroke, angered John, he had fled to his Irish estate to wait for John to come round. These and other incidents persuaded John he should deal with the barons in Ireland. So in 1210 John raised an army and a great fleet of ships, and in two months, conquered them all. On the way to and from Ireland he stayed at Margam Abbey in Glamorgan and nearly ruined them with the cost of feeding him and his men. It was made worse by the fact that William III de Breos was the Abbey's benefactor[xxxiv]. John took away the Lacy lands as punishment for sheltering William, and took William's lands for himself[xxxv].

He didn't catch William though, who managed to escape to Wales where he was sheltered by Llywelyn ap Iorwerth, Prince of Gwynedd[xxxvi]. This was surprising since Llywelyn was married to John's daughter Joan (known in Welsh as *Siwan*). William later escaped to France through his port of Shoreham, disguised as a beggar. In France William told his secret about the death of Arthur of Brittany, which spread like wildfire, doing yet more damage to John's reputation[xxxvii]. William's wife Maud and eldest son (William IV) were captured in Scotland, having been smuggled there from the north of Ireland. Many other family members were also rounded up.

William's wife and son were handed over to John, who locked them in a dungeon in Windsor Castle and left them to starve to death[xxxviii]. A horror story is told that when the dungeon was opened, William IV was sat upright in a chair with his mother embracing him and apparently kissing his cheek. When they looked closer, they found his cheek had been chewed away[xxxix]. Two of his son's children, John and Giles, were imprisoned at Corfe Castle in Dorset. Two others, Philip and Walter, were held at Angoulême in south-west France. They were not released until 1218, two years after King John's death[xl].

Most of the barons were becoming increasingly unhappy with John's unpredictable behaviour and incompetent rule, but his treatment of William III and his family was the final straw. Many came out in open rebellion, which led eventually to Magna Carta, the Great Charter by which they hoped to bring John into line.

William III died a beggar in Paris in 1211. Stephen Langton, the Archbishop of Canterbury, who was also in Paris taking refuge from John, arranged for his burial in the Abbey of St Victoire. He had wanted to be buried in St John's, Brecon, but it was not to be[xli].

Three of William's other children were Giles, Margaret and Reginald. Giles was Bishop of Hereford[xlii], Margaret married Walter de Lacy and Reginald married Grace Brewer. Margaret's marriage explains why the de Lacys helped William and his family when they fled to Ireland. Giles and Reginald swore vengeance for their family – which is where the Welsh come into the story.

Chapter 3 – The Kingdoms of Wales

Map of the Kingdoms of Wales

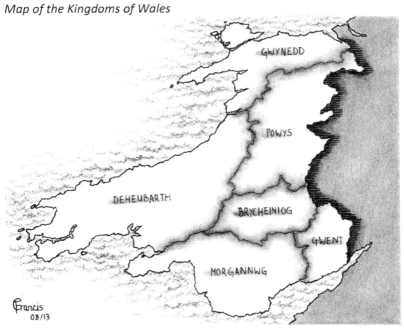

Until well into the 12th century, the Welsh still referred to themselves as *Britons*. They treasured a set of fables and myths proving the Welsh to be the earliest and prime people of the British Isles[xliii]. They never gave up on the dream of one day seeing the whole of Britain united again under their control, from London[xliv]. Later they called themselves *Cymry* – fellow countrymen.

Likewise with the Norman Marcher Lords - they weren't all Norman and they wouldn't have described themselves as Marcher Lords. Most of them had lands in England, often in Normandy and elsewhere in the Angevin empire, and would have considered their Welsh lands of minor importance. Most of these had been acquired as frontier extensions to their territories[xlv]. The de Breos family was an exception – their Welsh estates greatly outnumbered their other lands.

The relationship between the Marchers and the Welsh was often brutal and bitter, but at times both could see the benefit of short-term alliances. The Normans took advantage of the rivalries between factions and befriended whichever party was to their benefit. And the Welsh quickly learned to better themselves by service to the invaders[xlvi]. They even served as soldiers against their own countrymen.

In medieval times, Wales was never a country or a principality, but a collection of kingdoms ruled over by native princes. From time to time one prince would gain the ascendancy over a larger portion of land and become a force to be reckoned with by the English king. The main regions were Deheubarth in the south-west, Powys in the centre and Gwynedd in the north.

The difficulty in sustaining a kingdom in Wales was because of the inheritance tradition of partibility. When a leader died his lands were divided between all his sons, and illegitimate sons had the same right to inheritance as legitimate sons. Thus, over time, the lands ruled over would become smaller with each generation. What actually happened was that alliances were made and younger sons bought off, but it often didn't work, and they were constantly at war with each other to keep control of a larger portion of land[xlvii].

Amongst the Anglo-Normans the rule was primogeniture – inheritance went to the eldest legitimate son. Other sons had to be appeased with some lands, or went into the church, but even this didn't always work out, as we saw with King John.

The man Henry II dealt with was the Lord Rhys of Deheubarth. He is credited with the holding of the very first Eisteddfod in 1176 at Cardigan[xlviii], and the arts flourished during his reign. He was one of the greatest Welsh leaders of the 12th century[xlix], as Llywelyn would be in the 13th. After a power struggle, Henry realised Rhys was better as an ally. They made peace in July 1163[l], and they were allies until Henry's death. Deheubarth thrived and Welsh politics and culture all benefited from the Lord Rhys's stable rule. He forged links with Norman families to consolidate his position, including the marriage of his eldest son Gruffydd to Maud de Breos, William III's daughter[li]. In an attempt to secure the succession, Rhys helped Gruffydd capture his half-brother Maelgwyn. He handed him over to William III, who held him captive for three years[lii]. Rhys was the dominant ruling Welsh prince for more than forty years[liii], but on his death in 1197 there was a dispute between his numerous heirs. This resulted in Deheubarth being divided and losing its prominent position[liv].

By King John's time the power in Powys was Gwenwynwyn, who ruled from 1175. He too rose to prominence in his area, but only for a short while when the fortunes of Deheubarth and Gwynedd waned. He attempted to take advantage of Lord Rhys's death but was defeated by an English army at Painscastle on 13 August 1198[lv]. He refused however to join forces with Llywelyn, preferring to ally himself with King John[lvi], who used him as a pawn in controlling the Welsh.

Despite leading several raids, he was largely kept in check by the vast swathe of land belonging to William III de Breos, which ran along the Welsh border and deep into mid Wales. And behind Powys, in the north and west, was Gwynedd, ruled from Snowdonia. Several Norman expeditions over the years tried to subjugate it, but they were always faced with guerilla attacks from the mountains, and had never succeeded.

Gwynedd was the kingdom which came to prominence in John's reign, and its ruler was Llywelyn ab Iorwerth. When William III de Breos fell out of favour, Llywelyn sheltered him, and later helped his sons. As John's troubles grew in the rest of his kingdom and drew his attention away from Wales, Llywelyn took full advantage and captured land in Powys and Deheubarth. He came to be known as Llywelyn the Great (*Llywelyn Fawr*).

Chapter 4 - Llywelyn the Great: Master of the Power Play

Llywelyn & his coat of arms

Francis
08/13

Llywelyn ab Iorwerth's mother Marared was the daughter of a prince of Powys, so it's likely he was raised in Powys (since Gwynedd was not a safe place to be for someone with a claim to a share of the land). After his father died, there is evidence his mother married into a Shropshire Marcher family, the Corbets of Caux. This would mean he received some of his upbringing and education in the March. That would explain the skill with which he later dealt with Marcher lords and English politics[lvii].

In the 1190s Llywelyn emerged in Gwynedd as a threat to his uncles, who had taken power after the death of Llywelyn's father, soon after his birth. In 1194 he joined a family coalition and attacked his uncle Dafydd, the ruler of eastern Gwynedd. Having gained concessions, and eventually imprisoning Dafydd, Llywelyn gradually took over land in western Gwynedd as cousins died or were dispossessed[lviii]. His cousin's son Hywel, took over the remaining territory, but was a loyal supporter and ally of Llywelyn.

In 1197 both the Lord Rhys of Deheubarth and Owain Cyfeiliog of Powys died, sparking great changes in the political map of Wales. Llywelyn formed a brief alliance with the new king of southern Powys, Owain's son Gwenwynwyn, who was stronger than him at that time. Gwenwynwyn had a lot of influence and kinship ties which Llywelyn wanted to make use of. He was also involving himself in the civil war between the sons of the Lord Rhys in Deheubarth[lix].

By 1201 Llywelyn was established as Prince of Gwynedd and came to be known as Llywelyn Fawr: Llywelyn the Great. The sons of Gruffydd ap Rhys and Matilda de Breos, Owain and Rhys, looked to Llywelyn for protection when their father died in 1201[lx]. Bordered as his lands were by the Marcher lordships, Llywelyn realised he needed peaceful relations with his neighbours. He entered into negotiations with King John, and a treaty was drawn up allowing him to operate Welsh or English law in his lands in return for swearing fealty[lxi]. This was the first treaty between a Welsh prince and an English king. He had free reign to rule Gwynedd as he saw fit, unlike English barons who had to ask the king's permission for many things.

In 1205 Llywelyn's relationship with John was further enhanced when he married King John's beloved illegitimate daughter Joan. John also gave him the valuable manor of Ellesmere in Shropshire[lxii]. It has been speculated Joan was the granddaughter of Sibyl de Breos, William III's sister. Joan's mother Agatha Ferrers was likely John's mistress[lxiii]. This would be the first link between Llywelyn and the de Breoses, though he was allied with William's grandsons in Deheubarth. More importantly, this marriage brought him into the network of blood and marriage ties between the leading rulers throughout western Europe. His children would be the grandchildren of the current king of England and nieces and nephews of the next – John's son Henry.

When William de Breos and his family fled to Ireland away from John, Gwenwynwyn of Powys saw his opportunity to seize de Breos lands in mid Wales: Brecon, Builth, Elfael and Radnor. John was angry at this, since the lands were forfeit to him. He invited Gwenwynwyn to a meeting in Shrewsbury in October 1208 and promptly stripped him of his lands and locked him up. Llywelyn took the opportunity to expand his territory, conquering southern Powys[lxiv]. Unlike Gwenwynwyn, Llywelyn had no complaint from John when he took over Gwenwynwyn's lands[lxv].

Then he took northern Ceredigion and looked to Deheubarth, where the sons and grandsons of the Lord Rhys were still fighting for power. To reassure John of his loyalty, he accompanied him north on his expedition against the king of Scots in 1209. This was an almost unprecedented move, for a Welsh leader to travel so far from Wales[lxvi].

As with William III de Breos, Llywelyn's fall from John's grace was equally sudden. William escaped from John's expedition to Ireland back to Wales in the summer of 1210, and Llywelyn helped him. It may have been an excuse for raids of plunder, or Llywelyn may have seen the political wind was changing against John. All John's subjects felt threatened by his mercurial temper, unpredictable behaviour and paranoid nature. John's excessively harsh treatment of William, a man who had been so close to him, was a major factor in turning his barons against him.

In retaliation John restored Gwenwynwyn to Powys and supported Maelgwyn ap Rhys's attempts to recover Ceredigion. A large army was sent to north Wales, which was only halted by lack of supplies (in Gwynedd it was not possible for the army to live off the land). More seriously, John succeeded in attracting several of the Welsh princes previously loyal to Llywelyn. In the summer of 1211 the army marched again, better supplied and bigger than ever. They penetrated all the way to Bangor. Llywelyn realised he had no choice but to submit to John.

He sent his wife Joan, John's daughter, to negotiate. John imposed humiliating peace terms, and left Llywelyn with barely enough land to call himself a prince. He even had to promise his lands would revert to John if he failed to produce a male heir with Joan[lxvii]. The last Welsh princes to submit to John were Owain and Rhys of Deheubarth, William's grandsons[lxviii].

Within a year the other Welsh princes, shocked at the harshness of John's response, had transferred their allegiance to Llywelyn. In an astute political move, Llywelyn had also made alliances with King Philip of France and the Pope. War broke out in summer 1212. John responded by assembling a huge army from all over his empire, including a large force of labourers for castle-building. But news of English barons also joining Llywelyn caused John to pause and deal with his barons first. Two of those joining Llywelyn were Bishop Giles de Breos, who may have assisted in the pact with King Philip, and Reginald de Breos[lxix], sons of William III.

The attack on Llywelyn never took place because John had to turn to counter the threat of an invasion from France. That gave the Welsh room to conduct more raids and capture more castles. Llywelyn recovered all the lands he had lost and extended his reach south-wards. In 1213 Giles and Reginald de Breos regained all the lands they had previously held in the Welsh Marches[lxx].

Chapter 5 – Magna Carta & Civil War
Adaptation of the Runnymede crest

John then executed a master stroke against all his enemies: in March 1215 he made peace with the Pope, took the Cross and pledged to go on Crusade[lxxi]. This put all his lands under the pro-tection of the Pope, and any attack against him would be an affront to the Pope himself. This move, which was accepted after payment of a huge sum of money, also meant the interdict on England and John's excommunication would be lifted[lxxii].

John agreed to accept Stephen Langton as Archbishop of Canterbury and Langton, Bishop Giles de Breos and all churchmen were ordered back to England to absolve John's sins. They arrived at Dover in 1213 and met John at Winchester[lxxiii]. They had to obey the Pope despite their hatred of John – they didn't believe his repent-ance for a minute. He had lost widespread support among the churchmen as well as the barons.

John's situation went from bad to worse. His attempt to regain Normandy in 1214 was not a success, and his defeat at the battle of

Bouvines in July encouraged baronial opposition. John gave up his attempts to crush the Welsh and instead tried to win them over by releasing hostages and sending peace proposals. Llywelyn would have none of it, and strengthened his alliances with rebel barons, including the de Breoses. To cement the alliance, Reginald de Breos, now a widower, married Gwladys Ddu, one of Llywelyn's daughters, in 1215[lxxiv]. Reginald saw an opportunity to gain land for himself at the expense of his imprisoned nephew John, the true heir to the de Breos inheritance. Giles was no longer able to intervene, since he died in the same year[lxxv].

In 1215 Llywelyn took Shrewsbury, a key symbol of English power on the Welsh border. His confederates in South Wales took Narberth and Gower, capturing Swansea and five local castles. He joined them and took Carmarthen, Llanstephan, St Clears, Laugharne, Trefdraeth, Emlyn, Cardigan and Cilgerran. The conflict between John and the barons gave Llywelyn the opportunity to impose his rule on mid and south Wales as well as his traditional territories in the north[lxxvi]. He ensured Gower was returned to the de Breoses.

At the same time as Llywelyn moved on Shrewsbury, the dissident barons seized London. John had been outmanoeuvred. Within weeks the barons forced John to negotiate with them, and invited Llywelyn along. The negotiations led to the Great Charter, Magna Carta, which John was forced to sign, at Runnymede on 15 June 1215[lxxvii]. The uniqueness of the document was in laying out not only the rights of the church and the barons, but also of ordinary people[lxxviii]. It included three Welsh clauses: the return of lands and liberties which they had been unjustly deprived of, the return of hostages (including Llywelyn's son Gruffudd), and the cancellation of the unfair charters extorted from the Welsh princes[lxxix].

For those of us who know little of history, Magna Carta is held up as a great blow for democracy, and we may think once John signed, it was all over. The truth is very different. Within weeks John had persuaded the Pope to absolve him from any promises made, declaring the Charter illegal and unjust[lxxx]. Frustrated, the barons went to war again, but this time went one step further. They invited

King Philip's son Louis to take the throne of England, believing this would bring a French army to their aid.

Llywelyn wasn't part of this, but he made sure to take full advantage of the chaos in England to further his ambitions in Wales. He continued his campaign in the south, surprising the Norman barons by attacking in winter. The biggest prize was Carmarthen, which had been the centre of royal power in Wales for more than a century. His army included all the major Welsh princes, including Gwenwynwyn from Powys and William III's grandsons from Deheubarth. It marked the first time Llywelyn led all of Wales and the size of his army meant no Marcher lord dared to stand against him[lxxxi].

Taking advantage of his new position, in 1216 Llywelyn summoned all the Welsh princes to a council at Aberdyfi to settle once and for all the fighting over the inheritance of Deheubarth. His partition of the kingdom was accepted by the rival parties and stood until his death. It's likely the princes swore some kind of oath of allegiance or homage to him, since Gwenwynwyn went away and renounced any loyalty. He was encouraged to stand up to Llywelyn by King John, who was in no position to send him any assistance, and he died in exile later that year. Llywelyn immediately moved to occupy southern Powys[lxxxii].

Meanwhile, John was desperate for allies in his war with Louis' army, which had landed in England. He appeared on the Welsh border and tried to make peace with Llywelyn and Reginald de Breos. John offered Reginald all his Marcher lordships back, as a vassal of Llywelyn. They would have none of it.

In October 1216, John fell ill, possibly with food poisoning, and died suddenly. His son Henry was only nine years old, so the future of the throne of England was in the balance. Would the next king be Louis, the prince of France, or nine-year-old Henry, who would need a regent to manage the kingdom until he came of age? Llywelyn kept out of it and watched to see which way things would go[lxxxiii].

Chapter 6 - King Henry III & the de Breos Heirs
Peace between England & Wales?

The civil war was won by Henry III's forces in September 1217, with the French defeated and the Welsh offered peace. The Treaty of Lambeth which ended the war was not acceptable to the Welsh, but Reginald de Breos saw his chance to re-enter the fold, and transferred his allegiance from Llywelyn to the new king. Reginald was restored to favour and given back the Bramber estate. Angered by his son-in-law's defiance, Llywelyn captured Brecon and Swansea, handing Swansea over to Rhys Gryg of Deheubarth. Reginald de Breos was forced to surrender to Llywelyn and yield his Welsh territories. Rhys Gryg swept through Gower and ousted all the English, giving their lands to the Welsh[lxxxiv]. Reginald's nephews, Rhys and Owain, princes of Deheubarth, also rose up and captured Builth.

In March 1218 Llywelyn met with the king's representatives and agreed a much better settlement, known as the Peace of Worcester. He had to make concessions, including the return of the de Breos lands, but much of his territory was accepted. But, instead of paying homage to him, he was expected to ensure the other Welsh princes came and paid homage to the king. Unfortunately, only one did, but the crown decided to keep Llywelyn's friendship, and didn't make a fuss[lxxxv].

In 1218 Peter de Maulay, constable of Corfe Castle, was ordered for the third time to release William III's grandsons, John and Giles. This time he complied. John de Breos was twenty and as the eldest son, laid claim to the de Breos estates, some of which were held by his uncle Reginald. The lordships of Bramber and Barnstable came to him with no trouble, but his claim for the Welsh lordships was refused.

Since Reginald was out of favour with Llywelyn, John de Breos turned to him to aid him in his claim against his uncle. In 1219 Llywelyn ordered Rhys Grug to give John Gower, and in return John made an alliance with Llywelyn by marrying his daughter Margaret[lxxxvi]. For those who have read my book *Alina, The White Lady of Oystermouth*, John and Margaret were Alina's great-grandparents.

In 1221 John repaired Swansea Castle with Llywelyn's permission. In 1228 Reginald died and John finally became the main heir to the de Breos estates, which he was by birthright. He became lord of the three Marcher castles of Skenfrith, Grosmont and Whitecastle, but he lost these in 1230 to Hugh de Burgh[lxxxvii]. His main Welsh residence was Oystermouth Castle in Gower, but he died at Bramber in 1232, after falling and being dragged along by his horse[lxxxviii].

Llywelyn turned his thoughts to the succession in his own lands. When he had married King John's daughter Joan, he already had children by a mistress, including a son, Gruffudd. According to Welsh law, illegitimate sons had as much right to inherit as legitimate ones. But Llywelyn had promised King John only a son of Joan's would inherit, and that was Dafydd.

So he began the long process of getting Dafydd recognised as his heir and attempting to placate Gruffudd with lands of his own. He obtained formal recognition of Dafydd as his heir by King Henry in

1220, the Pope in 1223, and the chief princes of Wales in 1226. Dafydd did homage to Henry as heir to Gwynedd in 1229. A year later Llywelyn arranged a highly advantageous marriage between Dafydd and Isabel de Breos, daughter of William V, Reginald's son[lxxxix].

While the negotiations were progressing however, there was a major scandal caused by William V de Breos, father of the potential bride. In 1228 he had succeeded his father Reginald de Breos. During a campaign against another Marcher lord, Llywelyn had captured William, who was fighting on the lord's side. He was held for ransom for £2,000. William may have been wounded and tended by Llywelyn's wife and her maids. He was held for six months, and on his release gave his word he would never again bear arms against Llywelyn, and his daughter would marry Llywelyn's son.

Not only would this be a third (or fourth) tie between Llywelyn's family and one of the most prominent Marcher families, but it would bring the Lordship of Builth as a dowry and other potential lands when William died and his lands were split between his daughters. Even more important, William's wife Eva was the sister of William Marshal, Earl of Pembroke and Regent of England.

At Easter 1230, William visited Llywelyn's court to finalise the marriage arrangements and possibly to negotiate the release of the companions and servants who had been captured with him. One day William was discovered in Llywelyn's chamber in bed with Llywelyn's wife Joan, King John's daughter[xc].

It's not known how long the affair had been going on, but it's possible they fell in love when Joan tended William's wounds after he was captured. They were immediately separated and imprisoned. Within a month William was tried by a council of Llywelyn's lords and sentenced to death. He was hung publicly on 2 May 1230. Llywelyn, the astute politician, behaved as an outraged husband with no regard for the consequences[xci].

Joan was imprisoned for twelve months, but was later forgiven, so it seems there was genuine love between them[xcii]. But it should be remembered she was also the half-sister of the king.

27

There are those historians who say it was a conspiracy to falsely accuse and murder William. Indeed, it did mean his daughters would come into their inheritance. But it jeopardised the whole marriage arrangement, so if it was true, Llywelyn was playing a dangerous game. Most likely it was a genuine affair. Llywelyn was at great pains to convince Isabel's relatives the marriage should go ahead[xciii].

It's interesting the Crown said nothing about the incident, except a mention in a letter to Llywelyn which referred to the 'mischance that befell him'[xciv]. There was no mention of the fact he had taken it upon himself to try, judge and execute a subject of the Crown. In fact, he began to style himself 'Prince of Aberffraw and Lord of Snowdon'.

The marriage went ahead and William's lands were split between his four daughters and their husbands.

Conclusion

Broken baronial coronet

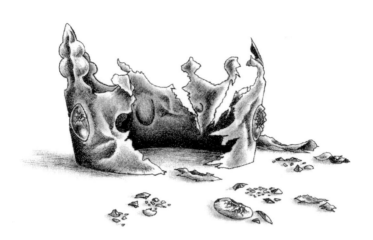

Francis
08/13

The old proverb says 'pride goes before a fall' and it was certainly true in William III de Breos's case. He rose to power through careful management of the estates he inherited and astute use of his favour with King John. But his dramatic rise was undone by disregard of payments due and the unguarded words of his wife. He over-reached himself and he and his wife thought they were invulnerable.

His fall had a huge effect on Welsh politics, because his vast swathe of lands in the Marches kept the power of the native princes in check. Without him, they were able to make advances that eventually led to Llywelyn ab Iorwerth having the power to negotiate with the king of England and be recognised as the supreme Welsh leader. By his skilful intervention in Marcher politics, Llywelyn was able to link his family to the de Breoses as their status revived and, through

William's granddaughter, to the English throne. Llywelyn's son and heir Dafydd married the niece of the regent of England.

King John's unpredictable and violent behaviour alienated the barons. He was not concerned with right and wrong, but saw justice as a tool for favouring his friends and attacking his enemies, and for raising revenue. The barons felt he tampered with justice in order to persecute them and trample on their inheritance rights[xcv]. His treatment of William III de Breos and his wife and son was the final straw that led to their rebellion.

William's remaining sons turned to Llywelyn for support in regaining their lands, giving Llywelyn the opportunities he needed. Even his own wife's affair with William's grandson didn't blind him to the advantageous marriage for his heir.

The great accumulation of lands and wealth gathered by William III de Breos, 4th Lord of Bramber, Lord of Gower and so much more besides, was created and broken in one generation. In the next generation they lost all their English lands except Bramber, and all their Welsh lands except Gower. William's grandson John was *only* Lord of Bramber and Gower.

If you enjoyed this book, why not leave a review online? Reviews are an author's lifeblood.

You might also enjoy the companion books:

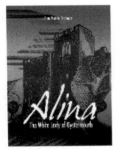

Alina, The White Lady of Oystermouth
The story of how a little rebellion by the heir to Gower ended up toppling Edward II from the English throne.

The Magna Carta Story: The Layman's Guide to the Great Charter
The layman's guide and a good story too. The relationships, arguments, bad behaviour, and civil war around the imposition of the Great Charter on King John, and what happened afterwards. Why is it considered so important after 800 years, and what did it actually say?

Fascinating stories from medieval Gower: battles, brutality, adultery, daring escapes, fairies and an ogre!
Witness the crimes of mad King John, the atrocities of the Ogre of Abergavenny and search for the lost treasure of Edward II.

All illustrated by the same talented artist.
Available in print and Kindle ebook from Amazon and in multiple ebook formats from Smashwords.com

Bibliography

Bartlett, Robert, *The Hanged Man*
Boulter, Matthew *The Career of William III de Briouze in the Reign of King John: Land, Power and Social Ties*
Carradice, Phil *Highlights of Welsh History*
Draisey, Derek *A History of Gower*
Erickson, Carolly *Brief Lives of the English Monarchs*
Evans, Edith *Swansea Castle and the medieval town*
Harris, Edward *Swansea*
Hobsbawm, Eric & Ranger, Terence (ed.) *The Invention of Tradition*
Jowitt, Susannah *The Movers & Shakers of Medieval England*
King, Edmund *Medieval England: From Hastings to Bosworth*
McLynn, Frank *Lionheart and Lackland: King Richard, King John and the Wars of Conquest*
Maund, Kari *The Welsh Kings: The Medieval Rulers of Wales*
Rees, David (ed.) *A Gower Anthology*
Rowlands, Ifor W *King John and Wales*, in Church, S D (ed.), *King John: New Interpretations*
Turner, Ralph V. *King John: England's Evil King?*
Turvey, Roger *Llywelyn the Great*
Turvey, Roger *Twenty-one Welsh Princes*
Walker, David, *Medieval Wales*

Online Resources:
http://freespace.virgin.net/doug.thompson/BraoseWeb/family/
http://freespace.virgin.net/doug.thompson/BraoseWeb/frames.htm
http://www.royal.gov.uk/HistoryoftheMonarchy/KingsandQueens ofEngland/TheAngevins/TheAngevins.aspx
http://steyningmuseum.org.uk/braose.htm
http://steyningmuseum.org.uk/braose2.htm
http://www.castlewales.com/dryslwyn.html

---

i
http://freespace.virgin.net/doug.thompson/BraoseWeb/family/william3.html
ii   Boulter, Matthew *The Career of William III de Briouze in the Reign of King John: Land, Power and Social Ties*

[iii] Erickson, Carolly *Brief Lives of the English Monarchs* p.67
[iv] Erickson, Carolly *Brief Lives of the English Monarchs* p.69
[v]
    http://www.royal.gov.uk/HistoryoftheMonarchy/KingsandQueensofEn
    gland/TheAngevins/TheAngevins.aspx
[vi] McLynn, Frank *Lionheart and Lackland: King Richard, King John and the Wars
    of Conquest* p.22
[vii] McLynn, Frank *Lionheart and Lackland: King Richard, King John and the Wars
    of Conquest* p.27
[viii]   C. Petit-Dutaillis & P. Guinard, *L'Essor des etats* d'Occident (Paris,
    1944), p.137 cited in McLynn, Frank *Lionheart and Lackland: King Richard, King
    John and the Wars of Conquest* p.290
[ix] McLynn, Frank *Lionheart and Lackland: King Richard, King John and the Wars
    of Conquest* p.34
[x] McLynn, Frank *Lionheart and Lackland: King Richard, King John and the Wars
    of Conquest* p.89
[xi] McLynn, Frank *Lionheart and Lackland: King Richard, King John and the Wars
    of Conquest* p.91
[xii] McLynn, Frank *Lionheart and Lackland: King Richard, King John and the Wars
    of Conquest* p.115
[xiii]   McLynn, Frank *Lionheart and Lackland: King Richard, King John and
    the Wars of Conquest* p.119-20
[xiv]   McLynn, Frank *Lionheart and Lackland: King Richard, King John and
    the Wars of Conquest* p.226
[xv] One mark was one third of a pound
[xvi]   McLynn, Frank *Lionheart and Lackland: King Richard, King John and the
    Wars of Conquest* p.265
[xvii]   King, Edmund *Medieval England: From Hastings to Bosworth* p.92
[xviii]   McLynn, Frank *Lionheart and Lackland: King Richard, King John and the
    Wars of Conquest* p.280
[xix]   Draisey, Derek *A History of Gower*, p.43
[xx] Bartlett, Robert *The Hanged Man*, p. 86
[xxi]
    http://freespace.virgin.net/doug.thompson/BraoseWeb/family/philip.
    html
[xxii]
    http://freespace.virgin.net/doug.thompson/BraoseWeb/family/willia
    m2.html
[xxiii]   http://steyningmuseum.org.uk/braose.htm; Walker, David *Medieval*

Wales p.51

xxiv

http://freespace.virgin.net/doug.thompson/BraoseWeb/frames.htm

xxv

http://freespace.virgin.net/doug.thompson/BraoseWeb/family/william3.html

xxvi

http://freespace.virgin.net/doug.thompson/BraoseWeb/family/william3.html

xxvii   Erickson, Carolly *Brief Lives of the English Monarchs, From William the Conqueror to Elizabeth II* p.73

xxviii   Harris, Edward *Swansea* p.14

xxix

http://freespace.virgin.net/doug.thompson/BraoseWeb/family/william3.html

xxx   Lands in Normandy: Briouze; Walter de Lacy's lands; Longueil near Rouen and other strategic sites surrounding Norman centres. Lands in England: Bramber in Sussex; half barony of Barnstaple; Stratton St Margaret & Berewick in Wiltshire; King's Arley in Staffordshire; Tetbury & Hampnett in Gloucester; Walter de Lacy's lands in Gloucestershire, Herefordshire & Shropshire; John of Torrington's estates in Devon; half the barony of Totnes; Shoreham in Sussex; land in Warwickshire & Leicestershire; Buckingham Castle; Paddington & half the village of Gomshall in Surrey; Winton in Dorset; temporary custody of the lands of Gilbert of Monmouth; the wardship of Walter de Beauchamp with lands in Warwickshire & Berkshire. Lands in Wales: Radnor & surrounding land; Builth; Brecknock; Abergavenny; Elfael; Kington; Glamorgan; Gower; Grosmont, Skenfrith & Llantilio castles in Gwent. Lands in Ireland: County, city & region of Limerick; Carrickfergus castle in Ulster; lands in Tipperary; castle of Knocgrafan; William de Burgh's lands in Munster. All are documented from original sources in Boulter, Matthew *The Career of William III de Briouze in the Reign of King John: Land, Power and Social Ties*

xxxi   McLynn, Frank *Lionheart and Lackland: King Richard, King John and the Wars of Conquest* p.307

xxxii   Turner, Ralph V *King John: England's Evil King?* p.169

xxxiii   http://freespace.virgin.net/doug.thompson/BraoseWeb/frames.htm p.12

xxxiv   http://freespace.virgin.net/doug.thompson/BraoseWeb/frames.htm p.14

xxxv   Turner, Ralph V *King John: England's Evil King?* p.107

xxxvi   McLynn, Frank *Lionheart and Lackland: King Richard, King John and the Wars of Conquest* p.338

xxxvii   http://freespace.virgin.net/doug.thompson/BraoseWeb/frames.htm p.13

xxxviii   http://freespace.virgin.net/doug.thompson/BraoseWeb/family/willia m3.html

xxxix   http://freespace.virgin.net/doug.thompson/BraoseWeb/frames.htm p.14

xl http://freespace.virgin.net/doug.thompson/BraoseWeb/family/william4.html

xli http://freespace.virgin.net/doug.thompson/BraoseWeb/family/william3.html

xlii   Rowlands, Ifor W *King John and Wales*, in Church, S D (ed.), *King John: New Interpretations* p.275

xliii   Hobsbawm, Eric & Ranger, Terence (ed.) *The Invention of Tradition* p.45

xliv   Davies, R R *History of Wales vol II, Conquest, Coexistence and Change: Wales 1063-1415* p.79

xlv   Davies, R R *History of Wales vol II, Conquest, Coexistence and Change: Wales 1063-1415* p.84

xlvi   Davies, R R *History of Wales vol II, Conquest, Coexistence and Change: Wales 1063-1415* p.101

xlvii   Davies, R R *History of Wales vol II, Conquest, Coexistence and Change: Wales 1063-1415* p.70

xlviii   Hobsbawm, Eric & Ranger, Terence (ed.) *The Invention of Tradition* p.56

xlix   http://www.castlewales.com/dryslwyn.html

l Davies, R R *History of Wales vol II, Conquest, Coexistence and Change: Wales 1063-1415* p.52

li http://freespace.virgin.net/doug.thompson/BraoseWeb/family/maud2.html

lii http://freespace.virgin.net/doug.thompson/BraoseWeb/frames.htm p.17

liii Davies, R R *History of Wales vol II, Conquest, Coexistence and Change: Wales 1063-1415* p.223

liv Walker, David *Medieval Wales* p.90

lv Davies, R R *History of Wales vol II, Conquest, Coexistence and Change: Wales 1063-1415* p.229

lvi Davies, R R *History of Wales vol II, Conquest, Coexistence and Change: Wales 1063-1415* p.236

lvii   Maund, Kari *The Welsh Kings: The Medieval Rulers of Wales* p.116

lviii   http://freespace.virgin.net/doug.thompson/BraoseWeb/frames.htm

p.17
[lix] Maund, Kari *The Welsh Kings: Warriors, Warlords and Princes* p.187
[lx] http://freespace.virgin.net/doug.thompson/BraoseWeb/frames.htm p.17
[lxi] Maund, Kari *The Welsh Kings: Warriors, Warlords and Princes* p.188
[lxii] Turvey, Roger *Twenty-one Welsh Princes* p.84
[lxiii] http://freespace.virgin.net/doug.thompson/BraoseWeb/frames.htm
p.17
[lxiv] Carradice, Phil *Highlights of Welsh History*, p.12
[lxv] Turvey, Roger *Llywelyn the Great* p.50
[lxvi] Maund, Kari *The Welsh Kings: Warriors, Warlords and Princes* p.192
[lxvii] Turvey, Roger *Llywelyn the Great* pp.54-6
[lxviii] http://freespace.virgin.net/doug.thompson/BraoseWeb/frames.htm
p.12
[lxix] Turvey, Roger *Llywelyn the Great* p.58
[lxx] Walker, David *Medieval Wales* p.50ff
[lxxi] Turner, Ralph V *King John: England's Evil King?* p.179
[lxxii] http://freespace.virgin.net/doug.thompson/BraoseWeb/frames.htm
p.14
[lxxiii] http://freespace.virgin.net/doug.thompson/BraoseWeb/frames.htm
p.15
[lxxiv] http://freespace.virgin.net/doug.thompson/BraoseWeb/frames.htm
p.16
[lxxv] Evans, Edith Swansea *Castle and the medieval town* p.6
[lxxvi] http://freespace.virgin.net/doug.thompson/BraoseWeb/frames.htm
p.16
[lxxvii] Turvey, Roger *Llywelyn the Great* p.61
[lxxviii]
http://www.royal.gov.uk/HistoryoftheMonarchy/KingsandQueensofEngland/TheAngevins/TheAngevins.aspx
[lxxix] Turvey, Roger *Llywelyn the Great* p.61
[lxxx] Turvey, Roger *Llywelyn the Great* p.62
[lxxxi] Turvey, Roger *Llywelyn the Great* p.64
[lxxxii] Turvey, Roger *Llywelyn the Great* p.64-6
[lxxxiii] Turvey, Roger *Llywelyn the Great* p.67
[lxxxiv] Turvey, Roger *Llywelyn the Great* p.72; Rees, David (ed.) *A Gower Anthology*, p.70
[lxxxv] Turvey, Roger *Llywelyn the Great* p.74
[lxxxvi] Turvey, Roger *Llywelyn the Great* p.76

lxxxvii
　　　　http://freespace.virgin.net/doug.thompson/BraoseWeb/family/john.h
tml
lxxxviii　　http://steyningmuseum.org.uk/braose2.htm
lxxxix　　Maund, Kari *The Welsh Kings: The Medieval Rulers of Wales* p.123
xc http://steyningmuseum.org.uk/braose2.htm
xci　　Turvey, Roger *Llywelyn the Great* p.90
xcii　　Turvey, Roger *Twenty-one Welsh Princes* p.90
xciii　　Turvey, Roger *Llywelyn the Great* p.92
xciv　　Calendar *of Close Rolls, 1227-31,* 368 cited in Turvey, Roger *Llywelyn the Great* p.92
xcv　　Turner, Ralph V *King John: England's Evil King?* p.166

Printed in Poland
by Amazon Fulfillment
Poland Sp. z o.o., Wrocław

54008632R00025